A WILDLIFE WATCHER'S FIRST GUIDE

Faces in the Mountains

RON HIRSCHI

Photographs by

THOMAS D. MANGELSEN

COBBLEHILL BOOKS/Dutton
New York

For Nichol and Scott — R.H.

For Dan Fulton — T.M.

Text copyright © 1997 by Ron Hirschi
Photographs copyright © 1997 by Thomas D. Mangelsen
Library of Congress Cataloging-in-Publication Data
Hirschi, Ron
Faces in the mountains/Ron Hirschi;
photographs by Thomas D. Mangelsen
p.   cm.—(A Wildlife watcher's first guide)
Summary: Focuses on animals that live in mountainous
regions of the United States, including grizzly bears,
marmots, bighorn sheep, and others.
ISBN 0-525-65225-6
1. Mountain animals—Juvenile literature.   [1. Mountain
animals.]   I. Mangelsen, Thomas D., ill.   II. Title.
III. Series: Hirschi, Ron.   Wildlife watcher's first guide.
QL113.H555 1997 599—dc20 95-48421 CIP AC
Published in the United States by Cobblehill Books,
an affiliate of Dutton Children's Books,
a division of Penguin Books USA Inc.,
375 Hudson Street, New York, New York 10014
Designed by Kathleen Westray
Printed in Hong Kong
First Edition   10 9 8 7 6 5 4 3 2 1

Willow ptarmigan

Mule deer

Moose

Today I went for a walk in the Rocky Mountains near where my family and I live in Montana. My dog stayed at home because it is spring and I didn't want her to scare animals. Birds are nesting and baby rabbits have just been born.

I saw a pair of golden eagles, some mule deer, and tracks of a moose near a beaver pond that is surrounded by aspen trees. I wonder what animals live in mountains near your home in the Adirondacks, Sierras, Cascades, or Great Smokies? What animal faces could we see from winter to spring, summer to fall? Can we ever see them all?

YOUR FRIEND,

Ron Hirschi

Visit the mountains with
your family and climb with
them way up into the clouds,
up where you can almost touch
the sky. Snow might fall on
these high mountain meadows,
even in summer. And long
after you have gone and winter
arrives, snow will cover the
ground for many months. Lots
of animals sleep then, until
spring wildflowers appear.

Teton Range, Grand Teton National Park

Grizzly bears sleep the winter away in their western mountain homes. They wake from their long naps, hungry as a bear can be. Fresh spring grass, fish, and many mammals big and small are their favorite foods. Once, grizzly bears lived on prairies and in lower valleys. But people have only left room for them in the high mountain forests where they can hide and find food and safe dens for sleeping.

Grizzly bear

Black bear

Black bears are the grizzly's smaller and darker relatives. They hunt ground squirrels and other animals in mountain meadows, but spend more time eating ants, berries, and wildflowers too.

Marmot

Marmots are smaller still. They whistle from the entrances of their burrow homes. They are furry like bears and they sleep in winter. Unlike the bears, marmots eat only plants and will let you walk quite near. But come only so close or the marmots will pierce the air with their shrill calls, warnings to their families that danger is near.

If you hike on the highest trails that lead to steep rock cliffs, you will see mountain goats. Their fluffy white fur and shiny black horns are unlike any other animal's. A goat might be chased by a mountain lion, one of its only predators, and it needs sharp horns for protection. But the goats living in our western mountains find more safety by climbing with great skill on the steepest rocks and ice.

Sometimes mountain rabbits are white. Sometimes they are brown. Changing coats with the seasons, the snowshoe hares can run fast as mountain breezes. And they can stop suddenly, standing so still, many predators will pass them by.

Snowshoe hare

Weasels change coats winter to spring too. Quick and fierce, they can catch rabbits and pikas twice their size. Because weasels are so long and slender, they can fit into small holes in the ground, between rocks, and inside fallen logs where they capture mice, beetles, and birds.

Long-tailed weasels

Bighorn sheep — ewe, lamb, and ram

Mountain sheep stand so still you may think
they are rocks from a distance. A Rocky Mountain
bighorn's soft brown coat helps it blend into

Dall sheep

summer meadows. Other sheep are white to match the snow. These are the Dall sheep of Alaska with horns that have beautiful sweeping curls.

Moose

Moose are much taller than sheep. As high as eight feet at the shoulders, they can wade in deep waters of beaver ponds or mountain lakes. Here they munch soft water plants. Moose also eat willow branches and the tips of pine trees when winter snow covers other plants.

Beaver

Elk are almost as big as moose. But their antlers are more like thin branches, not thick and flat like the huge moose headgear. You can also tell the two apart by coat color. Moose are dark chocolate, elk more milky brown. And though moose like to live alone, you may see elk in great herds of a hundred or more. Baby elk are known as calves and must beware of predators, especially grizzly bears that hide along the meadow edge.

Elk

Deer too must beware. The mule deer's ears seem big enough to scoop up all sounds. Its eyes are always alert. Watch its tail as it twitches. The black tip helps you know a mule deer from its relative, the whitetail deer. But the whitetail is rare in high mountains, preferring lower valleys or the willow-lined banks of streams.

Mule deer

Golden eagle

Mountain predators might dive from the air, quickly and suddenly. Watch for the largest of these birds, golden eagles, and the smaller falcons to swoop down and catch ground squirrels, rabbits, or birds.

Ground squirrels are especially important for these predators and if you spend time watching them, you will learn more about why they stand alert. They must watch out for danger from all directions.

Arctic ground squirrel

Mountain predators might leap from tall grasses, a burrow, or snowy cover. Coyote, fox, and wolf are quick and strong. All of these relatives of our pet dogs live in mountains. Wolves are biggest and rarest and can catch moose, elk, and deer. Coyotes are slightly smaller and eat many more small animals like mice and ground squirrels. Foxes are much smaller and skilled in sneaking up on tiny birds, mice, and frogs. Like the wolves and coyotes, they also eat berries.

Red fox

Gray wolf

Coyote

Mountain bluebird

Watch the treetops for mountain birds. The colorful mountain bluebird seems to wear a tiny piece of the summer sky. You will know the

Black-billed magpie

mountain chickadee when it calls its name. And
the magpie is best recognized by its long tail that
sparkles purple and green in the sun.

Western tanager

Tanagers and lazuli buntings might perch above your head in a pine, spruce, or aspen tree. Robins live in the mountains too. So does the crossbill with its beak just right for opening cones and snatching the seeds inside.

Lazuli bunting

Red crossbill

Raven flies far and wide, always searching the ground below for a meal to steal or a nest to rob.

Ptarmigan change colors by winter and spring, blending with the mountain weather and meadow colors. Their winter white feathers help them survive when snow and cold arrive. Their color change is one signal that winter is here — time for you and me to hike down from their snow-covered home.

Raven

Willow ptarmigan

Gray jay

In wintertime, many mountain birds will remain here in the high country. When marmots and bears sleep in the safety of their underground dens, the friendliest face in the mountains may appear. Always curious, the gray jay might even land on your fingertips. It is called camp robber by some because this jay will sneak food from your backpack. Maybe it searches too for its other mountain friends that will appear, as soon as spring returns.

Cliff swallows

Clark's nutcracker

White pelicans

Spotted sandpiper

Searching for More Faces

When you see one animal, chances are good that others will be nearby. And the animals you see together form a kind of community — even if some are predators and some are prey. Since many animals have the same kinds of needs, they will live together or nearby because of food, water, or shelter that is shared. Small birds flock together to help them avoid predators. Large mammals like the elk will do this too, gathering as a herd to avoid grizzly bears or wolves. No matter what the reasons, you might see some of the following animals together, so watch for each of them in their special communities in the high hills and mountains.

Grizzly bear, elk, moose, wolf, sandhill crane, Clark's nutcracker, white pelican, golden eagle, marmot, weasel, and coyote might be seen in the same area. A good place to see them all together is in the Lamar Valley of Yellowstone National Park.

Black bear, mule deer, skunk, marmot, ground squirrel, spotted sandpiper, raven, and magpie often live in the same valleys throughout western mountains.

Mountain goat, cougar, red fox, falcons, eagles, bobcat, fisher, and mountain bluebird share high peaks in the

Rocky Mountains and the coast ranges such as the mountains of Olympic and Mount Rainier national parks.

Mountain bighorn sheep, grizzly bear, Clark's nutcracker, raven, red fox, pika, coyote, badger, and ground squirrel live in our northern mountains of the West.

Black bear, white-tailed deer, crow, weasel, bobcat, coyote, red fox, and raccoon can be seen together in eastern mountains such as those of the Great Smokies.

Mountain bluebird, mule deer, javelina, cougar, and falcons can be found in the southern mountains such as at Big Bend National Park.

Ptarmigan, elk, mule deer, mountain sheep, lazuli bunting, tanager, flicker, kestrel, pika, weasel, and black bear live together in the Rocky Mountains, including the scenic areas of Colorado in Rocky Mountain National Park.

Moose, beaver, muskrat, white-tailed deer, woodcocks, and many owls can be seen in mountains of the northeastern United States, especially in Maine.

The mountains of North Carolina and Kentucky are now home to red wolves as well as deer, black bear, bobcat, owls, and many hawks.

Pika

Raccoon

Great gray owl

Grizzly bears

Moose

Golden eagle

Mountain Facts

Grizzly bears hibernate in winter, and mother bears give birth to their tiny cubs at this time. Even though full-grown grizzlies might weigh more than 1,000 pounds, the newborns weigh only one pound.

Black bears can be brown, black, cinnamon, and even spotted with white fur. A large black bear may weigh 500 pounds.

Marmots are related to other burrow diggers, including the much more common groundhog that lives at lower elevations.

Mountain goats' hooves are soft and rubbery on the bottoms, helping them grip steep and slippery rocks.

Snowshoe hares are one of the most important prey animals in many mountains. They are food for bears, bobcats, lynx, and people too.

Bighorn sheep use their horns for battle and for scratching an itch on themselves or others. Their horns are permanently attached, growing bigger each year.

Moose, elk, and deer shed their antlers each year, growing new and larger sets in spring. Shed antlers are nibbled on by coyotes, mice, and ground squirrels. Like milk in our diet, the antlers are a good source of calcium.

Golden eagles and falcons can share the same skies, in

part because they eat different foods. The eagle prefers mammals, and some falcons eat only birds, while others eat mostly insects.

Mountain-dwelling wild dogs shed their heavy winter fur each spring, growing a new and thick coat the next fall. All have their special needs, but the wolf must have the largest living space. A wolf must travel many miles to find enough food for itself and a wolf pack might wander hundreds of miles each year.

Mountain bluebirds nest in tree cavities, often those abandoned by woodpeckers. These same nesting places are also used by chickadees.

Tanagers and buntings eat many kinds of insects, including caterpillars that might otherwise destroy mountain forest trees.

The ptarmigan is related to the prairie chicken and to grouse that live in woods far below the high mountains. Its feathered feet are just right for walking on snow.

Gray jays will be watching you if you picnic in the mountains, so watch for them and watch your sandwich!

Magpies build bulky stick nests low in trees or shrubby willows. Relatives of crows and ravens, they adapt well to new ways of finding food and shelter.

Gray wolf

Rock ptarmigan

Gray jay

Tips to Help You Find Animals in the Mountains

Search at the change in seasons, watching for feather and fur to turn from summer golden to winter white.

Listen to the wind, watching hawks, eagles, and falcons swoosh past mountain peaks in search of quiet valleys.

Follow the tracks of elk and deer to see calves and fawns that will be watching you too.

Follow mountain streams where deer, bluebirds, and others will come for a sip of cold water.

Mountain wildflowers are beautiful to look at. They are also food for wildlife. Watch the meadows for baby birds nibbling blossoms or bears munching leaves and grasses.

Find an aspen tree. Look for a hole in its soft wood. Here may be a nest of woodpeckers or smaller birds. Deer, elk, and moose will often rest in the shade of aspen trees.

Search for burrows. The biggest belong to bears, the smallest to chipmunks and ground squirrels. For safety, make sure you watch from a safe distance and in the company of a parent or, if you can, with the help of a ranger or other mountain guide.

Mountain lakes are fun for fishing and hold the cleanest, clearest water on earth. Eagles, osprey, and white pelicans hunt for fish on some of our largest high lakes, including the largest mountain lake of all, Yellowstone Lake. Along its shores you will find almost all the animals mentioned in this book.

No matter if you are in the wilderness of Montana or in the hills near your home, always hike with parents or other adults responsible for your safety. Let others know where you are at all times — mountains are beautiful but dangerous since weather changes quickly, hillsides are steep, and some animals can be very dangerous. Always keep a safe distance for your safety and the safety of all others.